STRENGTH OF THE HEART

MARCUS ALLEN'S
LIFE'S LITTLE PLAYBOOKS

Can't *is the worst word*
that is written or spoken.

—Edgar Guest

STRENGTH OF THE HEART

by Marcus Allen
and Carlton Stowers

Andrews McMeel
Publishing

Kansas City

00 01 02 03 04 TWP 10 9 8 7 6 5 4 3 2 1

www.andrewsmcmeel.com

Library of Congress Cataloging-in-Publication Data
Allen, Marcus, 1960–
    Strength of the heart / by Marcus Allen and Carlton Stowers.
          p. cm.
        ISBN 0-7407-0017-0 (hardcover)
        1. Allen, Marcus, 1960–   . 2. Football players–United States Biography.
    3. Youth–United States–Conduct of life. I. Stowers, Carlton. II. Title.
GV939.A54A55 1999   99-21801
796.332'092–dc21   CIP

Design by Holly Camerlinck

ATTENTION: SCHOOLS AND BUSINESSES

Andrews McMeel books are available at quantity discounts with bulk purchase for educational, business, or sales promotional use. For information, please write to: Special Sales Department, Andrews McMeel Publishing, 4520 Main Street, Kansas City, Missouri 64111.

This book is for Harold and Gwen Allen,
my mother and father; my teachers and advisers;
my friends and my heroes.
—M.A.

And for Anson and Ashley, Guy, and Andy.
—C.S.

CONTENTS

INTRODUCTION:

A MESSAGE TO MOM AND DAD

LISTEN CLOSELY TODAY, and you will hear the same story told over and over.

The world of sports, once the place we counted on for shining examples of determination and confidence, courage and unselfish teamwork, no longer provides the role models the youth of America can look up to.

Parents read news reports of highly paid athletes who give out autographs only if their fans are willing to pay for them and sadly remember a time when it wasn't that way. The modesty they once saw on the playing field is gone, replaced by end-zone celebrations and foul-language interviews they find embarrassing. They see stories of a star player being arrested for drug use or driving under the influence of alcohol and think of the poster of that athlete hanging in their child's room. And they wonder how to explain that just because someone can run fast, score touchdowns, or sink a game-winning basket, that person isn't to be judged a hero.

As one who has followed and written about sports for many years, I must admit

1

that the worry of parents is justified. I too am disappointed by much of what I see today. At the same time, I feel an obligation to point out that heroes still play the games we love so much. That is what this book is about.

Marcus Allen, a National Football League superstar for sixteen years, accomplished everything an athlete dreams of. In high school he played on championship teams, was named to several schoolboy All-America teams, and honored as the best athlete in the state of California. As a college student at the University of Southern California, he was again an All-American, set a lengthy list of NCAA rushing records, and won the Heisman Trophy. In the pros, playing first for the Oakland and Los Angeles Raiders and then for the Kansas City Chiefs, he continued to set remarkable records. He led the Raiders to victory in Super Bowl XVIII and was named the game's Most Valuable Player. He won Rookie of the Year and Player of the Year honors, was named to All-Pro and Pro Bowl teams, and scored more rushing touchdowns than any other player in the history of the NFL. Routinely throughout his career, his leadership abilities earned him the vote of his peers to serve as captain of the

teams on which he played. And he's a cinch to be selected to the Pro Football Hall of Fame, now that his playing days are over.

Pretty impressive, you'll agree. I can't think of another athlete more respected or with a greater list of accomplishments.

Yet to fully understand the athletic greatness of Marcus Allen, it is necessary to consider those things he wasn't. While obviously talented, he wasn't the biggest or strongest running back ever to put on a uniform. Nor was he among the fastest who played the game.

There were never any end-zone dances for the television cameras after he scored a touchdown, no self-serving bragging to sportswriters in the locker room afterward. For Marcus, personal achievements were important only if they helped his team to win.

Aside from the athletic ability and the love of sports he discovered on playgrounds and Little League fields as a youngster growing up in San Diego, Marcus's nearly unbelievable achievements are the result of far more than talent. At an early age he dedicated himself to the task of becoming the best he could be. He had the courage to take the right path toward his goals. And he developed a powerful belief in himself and those who offered him help and guidance.

The greatest value of athletics, he says, is that it is a mirror, a reflection of all the things one can expect to encounter in life. Sports offers a classroom in which any youngster—boy or girl, greatly talented or less than gifted—can discover the importance of teamwork and fair play, enjoy the thrill of winning, learn how to accept the disappointment of defeat—and, along the way, gain valuable knowledge of things like sacrifice and courage, leadership and loyalty.

These are the lessons Marcus Allen learned. That he now wishes to share them in his series of Life's Little Playbooks bears witness to the kind of person he is and stands as positive proof that heroes and role models are still among us.

—Carlton Stowers

The Encanto Braves—
Manager/Sponsor, Red
Allen (Marcus's dad);
Team Mother, Gwen
Allen (Marcus's mom)

Marcus as a little boy

LISTENING TO THE VOICES OF EXPERIENCE

1

IT WAS MANY YEARS AGO, but I still remember it as though it were yesterday.

A good friend of mine, who had played countless games with me in the neighborhood park and on the school playground, knocked at our front door one spring day. He was proudly dressed in the uniform of the Little League team he had just joined. Instead of the jeans and T-shirt that were our standard dress for playground games, he wore a shirt with a real number on it, pants that looked just like what the big leaguers wore, and a brand new cap that had the insignia of his team above the bill. I was impressed. I wasted no time asking my father if I, too, could play Little League baseball.

To my delight, Dad not only said yes but volunteered to sponsor and coach a team. This was my introduction to organized sports.

Though it may seem like bragging to say so, we had a very good team, mostly because my father was a fine coach. He patiently explained the fundamentals of the game, corrected our awkward batting stances, and talked endlessly about the importance of teamwork. Above all, he told us, the game should be fun.

But while I listened and learned, I was convinced that I was not at the position I would play best. Though my father put me at shortstop, I saw myself as a star center-fielder like Willie Mays, making long runs to catch the deep fly balls of opposing bat-ters. As the season went on I became more and more sure that I should be in center field. But I couldn't talk my dad into giving me a chance. I brought it up at the dinner table in the evenings, tried to talk to him about it in the mornings when he was get-ting ready to go to work, but with no luck. "We need you at shortstop," he said. End of conversation.

So, in my twelve-year-old wisdom, I came up with a plan. I began to organize a strike, urging my teammates to agree that they would not play any more if I wasn't immediately moved to center field. When I finally had the backing of everyone on the team, I went to my father and boldly told him of our decision.

He listened to what I had to say with-out any sign of anger or disappointment. Then, when I'd finished, he began slowly to collect the bats and balls and put them in a bag. "Well," he said at last, "I guess the season is over."

You won't be surprised, I'm sure, to learn that the support of my teammates collapsed immediately. They wanted to play. I did too. So the Great Little League Player Strike ended as quickly as it had begun.

I stayed at shortstop, and by the end of the summer we had won the league championship. To my surprise, I was picked for the All-Star team.

More important, I had taken my first step toward understanding what teamwork means. In his quiet way, my father showed us—me in particular—that no one player is more important than the team and the goal it is trying to achieve.

Still, I must admit, the learning process was slow. My stubborn streak showed again when I played football for Lincoln High School.

My first real hero was my older broth-er, Harold. Watching him make tackle after tackle from his middle linebacker position convinced me that I too wanted to be a defensive player once I got the opportunity to try out for the high school team.

On the long-awaited day I reported to varsity Coach Vic Player, I explained right away that I wanted to be a defensive back.

The Allen Family: Parents—Harold and Gwen; Children—Harold Jr., Michael, Damon, Michelle, and Marcus

on Coach Player's team, you were expected to learn about sportsmanship and fair play. You made your grades or you were history. If you drank or smoked or experimented with drugs, he didn't want you around.

"If you play for me," I remember him telling us, "I become like your father, and I treat each of you as if you were my son. I make the rules. All I ask is that you follow them."

When the season opened in my sophomore year, I was in the starting lineup as the Hornets' free safety. I can't tell you how happy and proud I was.

By the end of my junior year I had been picked for the all-league defensive team. In one game I made forty tackles, and the local paper ran my picture. I must admit I was feeling pretty good about myself—until Coach Player called me into his office.

Holding the newspaper, he congratulated me on my performance and even admitted he was glad I had received some recognition for my efforts. But he had

He assured me I would get a chance to prove I had the talent for the job.

Looking back over my athletic career, I know now how lucky I was to play for so many outstanding coaches. Vic Player is high on that list. He made it clear that he expected everyone to work hard, pay attention, and do what he said. Any athlete who wasn't willing to follow his list of strict rules was quickly told to turn in his uniform and not waste everyone else's time. If you were another message. "Marcus," he said, "I believe you have the ability to be an outstanding player. And I'll do everything I can to help you become as good as you can be. But you must learn that we have no stars on this team. No matter how many tackles you make, you are no more important than anyone else. I want you to remember that. If you continue to work hard and improve—and keep in mind that you are a part of a team effort—you'll be playing college football in a couple of years."

Coach Player was telling me the same thing my father had when he'd begun bagging up the Little League equipment, refusing my childish demand to play another position. Neither man had room for a player who places himself above the others on a team.

Some facts of life, however, are learned slowly. I'd like to say that the things my coaches were teaching me made perfect sense, and I immediately began to live by their rules. The truth is, I had more learning to do.

As my senior year approached, there was a strong feeling that we were going to be one of the best teams Lincoln High had ever produced. The only real problem was that our starting quarterback had gradu-

ated. As spring training neared, Coach Player told me I was going to fill that vacancy.

Quarterback is the dream position of almost every football player, but it was never mine. I was a defensive back, and that's all I wanted to be. I made my feelings known. I begged the coach to find some other quarterback and let me continue as the team's free safety.

"You're going to do both," he replied. "We have a good chance to win a lot of games this season, but only if we have a quarterback who can move the ball for us. You're going to be that person."

The plan was for me to spend my senior season as a two-way starter, at free safety and at quarterback. I should have felt flattered. I should have been excited.

Instead, when spring training began, I did everything I could to convince the coach that I wasn't the quarterback he was looking for. In practice I fumbled snaps on purpose. I took my time getting into position for passes and threw a lot of interceptions. I loafed, pouted, and kept asking to be allowed to report to the other end of the field, where the defense was going through their drills.

Finally, Coach Player's patience ran out. One afternoon he stopped practice and walked over to where I was standing. It didn't take a genius to see he was very angry. "If you're not going to try," he yelled at me, "then get out of here." And he pointed toward the dressing room.

I had been thrown off the team.

That evening I rushed home to tell my father what had happened. I was certain he would be outraged. He knew I was an all-league defensive back. The team needed

Marcus playing high school football

me. Surely he would phone the coach and demand that I be allowed to return.

Things didn't go as I expected.

Coach Player had already called to explain what had happened. Instead of being upset, my father didn't seem at all interested in coming to my rescue. "What did you say to the coach?" I finally asked.

"I told him the problem was between the two of you," he said. "Don't you have some homework to do?"

Later that evening I approached him again. "Do you think the coach would let me back on the team if I promise to try harder to be a good quarterback?"

"Son," he said, "That's up to the coach."

In six words he was telling me the problem was one I had created. I would have to be the one to solve it.

The following morning I went directly to Coach Player's office and apologized. I prom-ised I would try my hard-est to become the best quarterback I could be if he would give me another chance. That afternoon I was allowed to return to the team. To my great relief, my football career had not ended.

Coach Player's prediction came true. In my senior season we scored 500 points, setting a new county record, and our defense allowed fewer points than any other in the league's history. We went into the play-offs undefeated. And though I didn't exactly consider myself to be the next Joe Montana or John Elway, I was really enjoying my role as the team's quarterback. It was fun to play both offense and defense.

We were the smallest school to make it into the play-offs. Each week we were the underdogs, but each week we managed to win and finally advanced to the county championship game. We began hearing reports that as many as 25,000 people would be in San Diego's Jack Murphy Stadium to watch us play Kearney High.

The sportswriters were quick to compare the match to David against Goliath. Kearney was a bigger school. It had more players on its roster and was also undefeated. No one seemed to think we had a chance.

We beat them 34–6. Everything we did that night seemed to work perfectly. Early in the game I broke loose down the sidelines and ran 85 yards for my longest touchdown of the season. Then I had runs of 30, 20, and 10 yards for touchdowns. Finally, I intercepted a Kearney pass and returned it 60 yards for a fifth touchdown. Someone told me later that I had accounted for 317 yards during the game.

At the final gun the celebration began. Fans were cheering, the band played, cheerleaders were chanting, "We're Number One." Coach Player slapped me on the back and smiled. "Not bad for someone who didn't want to play offense," he said. "Not bad at all."

As I mingled with my teammates, I saw my father climb out of the stands. I began to run to meet him, but a security guard stopped him, saying no one was allowed on the field except players and coaches.

He pointed in my direction. "That's my son," he said. Even from a distance I could hear the pride in his voice. The guard smiled and waved my dad onto the field. He hugged me, and I could tell he was crying. "I'm so very proud of you," he whispered.

I had never felt better in my life.

In the days that followed our championship victory, I was treated like a hero.

And, yes, I enjoyed it. But the real heroes were the two men who had shown they cared enough about me—as a person and as an athlete—to teach me valuable lessons I would never forget.

My father had been right to refuse to let me decide what position I would play on his Little League team. Winning the league championship was not as important to him as showing his son that teamwork and respect for authority are worth more than any trophy. Coach Player proved his point when he dismissed me as starting defensive back because I didn't understand the importance of doing what was best for the team. Making me learn that was even more important to him than winning.

Believe me, I've never known a coach who doesn't want to win, but the really great ones look upon their jobs as something more. Coach Player was determined

Marcus's school picture, age 11

to see that the boys who played for him learned the rules of life that would help them become good, right-thinking men.

I've often looked back on those days and wondered what my life would have been like had he not cared enough to allow me a second chance. What if he had not let me return to the team? I would never have experienced the thrill of winning that county championship. No college recruiter would have ever knocked on my door. The Heisman Trophy that sits in my den would belong to someone else. I would never have had the rare thrill of playing in a Super Bowl or any of the other wonderful experiences I had during my career as a professional football player.

None of those things would have ever happened had I not had people who so willingly took time to offer the guidance that pointed me in the right direction.

2 FAMILY VALUES

IF THERE IS ONE PERSON I have admired and looked up to more than any other in my life, it is my father. He has always been a bigger-than-life figure to me.

He grew up on a farm in Texas and became head of the family at age eleven when his father died, helping his mother raise his younger brothers and sisters. At a time when most kids his age were enjoying a carefree life, my father was learning the lessons of responsibility, hard work, and personal sacrifice. He had to drop out of school and take a job. Once a promising athlete himself, he had little time to participate in sports.

Making certain there was food on the table was more important than scoring touchdowns or hitting home runs. My father had to learn a lot of lessons the hard way. And he passed them on to us.

If a person is to be successful in life, he would say, it is important to make the right decisions along the way. To be good citizens we had to understand the difference between right and wrong and respect the rights of others. My father called them his "life lessons," and he talked about them often. So did my mother.

Together, they were a great team. They taught us. They offered advice and guidance. And they gave each of us loving support and encouragement.

They saw to it that we understood the importance of education and discipline. They wanted us to sample everything good that life had to offer. We sang in the choir on Sundays, attended Boy Scout meetings, and took music lessons. We learned quickly that homework was to be done before we

Marcus's dad, Harold Allen, and Marcus's mom, Gwen Allen (left)

went out to play. If we broke rules like these, my parents constantly reminded us, there would be a price to pay.

This would be true throughout our lives, they explained, even after we left home and became adults. They knew everyone who expects to be a success in today's society must accept the fact that rules are a necessary part of life.

Everything we did, everything we were involved in, was viewed by my parents as a learning experience. When my father traveled throughout the county to the construction sites where he was working, he would often load us into the pickup and take us with him. Why? He wanted us to learn about the world beyond our own neighborhood.

In all honesty, I must admit I did not see the value of everything my parents tried to teach me. For instance, they wanted me to learn to play the piano. My father would drop me off at the teacher's house once a week, promising to return and pick me up when my lesson was completed.

I had other ideas—as my parents learned when the teacher explained that she didn't feel right accepting payment for lessons I wasn't actually taking. What I had been doing was waiting until my father drove away and then running over to a nearby park to play baseball. I was careful to be waiting in the teacher's front yard when he came back to pick me up.

When my father realized I was not actually having the lessons, he quit taking me. I knew he was disappointed, so I was surprised when my only punishment was a stern lecture about lying.

Now I know he had decided to allow me to learn the reason by myself. I always loved music and, as I grew older, found

myself regretting that I did not take advantage of the lessons he had paid for. So when I signed to play professional football with the Oakland Raiders, the first thing I did with my bonus check was to buy a piano and hire a teacher. My father had been right all along. It was one of the smartest and most enjoyable things I've ever done.

I remember Dad coming home one evening with a drug identification kit he had borrowed from a friend in the police department. He and Mother sat us at the kitchen table. Carefully, they described what marijuana and cocaine and heroin looked like. They explained the effects these drugs could have on a person's mind and body. The message was clear. There was only one choice when it came to drugs and alcohol: Stay away from them.

If we saw people drinking or using drugs at a party, we were told to leave and come home. "Don't even drink the punch," my father warned, "because someone may have decided it would be a 'cool' idea to spike it with alcohol. And stay out of rest rooms. That's where people hide to smoke a joint or snort cocaine."

The best way to deal with problems, he explained to us, was before they occurred, not after.

It is one of the most important things my father ever taught me. I've seen alcohol claim the lives of friends and teammates. I've watched promising athletic careers end too soon because of drug addiction. Were they ever warned of the dangers they faced? If they were, why didn't they listen?

Marcus with his brother Damon, who plays for the B.C. Lions in the Canadian Football League

I was lucky. I had people in my life who cared enough about me to explain the dangers of getting involved in drinking or using drugs.

The Allen Brothers: Michael, Harold Jr., Damon, Marcus, and Darius

STRENGTH OF THE HEART

3. HEROES

OBVIOUSLY, SPORTS WAS A BIG THING for all the Allen children. But not because our parents pushed us into joining teams. We played football and basketball and baseball because it was fun. And, like all kids, we did our best to run and throw like the star players we watched on television.

In baseball season we would draw chalk baselines in the backyard and do our best to mimic the games we'd watched. I tried to be Roberto Clemente of the Pittsburgh Pirates. If we had seen a professional football game that was played in the mud,

we would water down the yard before getting our game under way so we could get as wet and dirty as those we wanted to be like. I was Leroy Kelly, the tough-running fullback of the Cleveland Browns. When the season changed to basketball I became Walt Frazier of the New York Knicks or Jerry West of the Los Angeles Lakers, driving the lane in our driveway.

But as I grew older, I realized that to earn my real admiration, these players had to have more than the ability to run fast, score touchdowns, or get the game-winning hit. The way they lived their lives was every bit as important as their athletic talent. To me, sports' true heroes are those who are determined not only to prove themselves the best but to make the world around them a better place.

For instance, how did Jackie Robinson, the great third baseman for the Brooklyn Dodgers, deal with the pressures of being the first black man allowed to play major league baseball?

Back in 1947, when Dodgers owner Branch Rickey decided it was high time for baseball to be integrated, he knew he had to select a special person. Not only did this man have to be a remarkable player, he had to have the courage and character to deal with being an unwelcome black in what was then an all-white world.

How could someone concentrate on playing ball with a storm of controversy always swirling around him? Jackie Robinson heard angry curses and death

JACKIE ROBINSON

Jackie Robinson played for the Brooklyn Dodgers from 1947 to 1957. He helped the Dodgers win six National League pennants and the 1955 World Series. He was elected to the Baseball Hall of Fame in 1962.

threats yelled at him from the stands every day. He was not even allowed to stay in hotels or eat in restaurants with his fellow players when the team traveled around the country. How many times did he consider just walking away from it all, leaving to someone else the task of breaking down these ugly barriers?

No athlete has left a greater legacy than Jackie Robinson, and not just because he became one of baseball's superstar players. What he did for others is his most memorable accomplishment, greater than the championships he helped the Dodgers to win. Robinson knew the hopes and dreams of future generations of young blacks rode on his shoulders. He courageously opened doors that later athletes like Marcus Allen would be able to walk through and feel welcome.

Jackie Robinson was not the only black athlete to triumph over racial prejudice.

Jesse Owens earned the admiration of fans around the world by winning four gold medals at the 1936 Olympic Games in Berlin, Germany. Owens performed his history-making feat as Adolf Hitler, the powerful German leader who preached that whites were superior to blacks, watched in anger. Hitler even refused to shake the hand of this record-setting American sprinter, who had won the 100-meter and 200-meters runs and the long jump and was on the winning four-man U.S. 100-meter relay team.

Later, when the United States was at war with Hitler and the Germans, boxing champion Joe Louis was matched against German fighter Max Schmelling and won the world heavyweight championship. Louis, who had grown up in the poorest black section of Detroit, was suddenly in a position of fighting for more than his own glory. The hopes of every patriotic American rested on his shoulders. He fought not only to show that his country had the best heavyweight fighter in the world. He fought to show that those who believed one person was inferior to another just because of skin color were wrong.

What Jesse Owens and Joe Louis did went far beyond their victories on the track and in the ring. They were black athletes who represented their country in a fight against the propaganda of a white racist dictator. Their talent and courage and class won the admiration of millions, and the importance of their accomplishments will forever be remembered.

Every time I play a round of golf I'm reminded of the seemingly endless battles fought by Charles Sifford. This black man, who had taught himself to be a first-class player, was not allowed to compete against the best white golfers in the world because of a rule that refused blacks membership in the Professional Golfer's Association. There were courses throughout the country where he was not allowed to play, simply because of the color of his skin. But Sifford, a man who believed in his own skills and his rights as an American citizen, refused to give up. Finally, through his determined efforts, the unfair rule was changed.

Black players, from Masters champion Tiger Woods to duffers like me, owe a big debt of gratitude to Sifford's determination. His battle was fought not just for his own

JESSE
OWENS

Jesse Owens was one of the most successful track athletes of all time. At various times he held world records in sprints, hurdles, and hurdle jumping. On one day—May 25, 1935—he set three world records and tied one more.

STRENGTH OF THE HEART

right to compete but for the rights of generations to come.

No athlete in modern history has had a more powerful effect on me than heavyweight champion Muhammad Ali. As a youngster, I can remember listening to his fights on the radio, bouncing around my bedroom, arms flailing, doing my best to imitate the style and grace he displayed in the ring.

He captured the sports world's imagination like no one else. The public, black and white, marveled at his talent and his confidence. He was the best-known, most-applauded athlete in the world. Then, at the height of his popularity, everything came crashing down. A devout Muslim, he refused to join the armed services when drafted. To do so, he said, would violate his religious beliefs. Suddenly he was

JOE LOUIS

Louis held the world heavyweight boxing Championship longer than any other boxer. He won 25 times and scored 20 knockouts before retiring in March 1949.

CHARLES SIFFORD

Sifford won five consecutive National Negro Championships from 1952-1956. He was the first African-American to win a major PGA tournament, the Hartford Open in 1967.

looked on as a traitor and a coward. Boxing officials took his title away. He was sentenced to serve time in jail. Yet Ali stood his ground, so strong in his beliefs that he was willing to risk the loss of once-admiring fans and the millions of dollars he would have earned as the greatest fighter in history. None of those things were as important to him as his personal beliefs.

Could I have done it? Would I have had the courage to risk everything I'd worked for all my life? I only wish I could say yes, I have this rare inner strength and conviction.

The one thing that sets the role model apart is courage. I'm not talking about someone willing to take great physical risks. I'm not even talking about the player who is praised for going into the game despite being injured. I'm talking about the courage to stand up for what is right and be willing to risk one's own future for the benefit and betterment of others.

Curt Flood, the great centerfielder of the St. Louis Cardinals, was such a person. One of the best players in the game, Flood was suddenly traded, going from St. Louis to the Philadelphia Phillies. It wasn't a move he wanted to make, but one of baseball's long-standing rules—called the reserve clause—left him no choice. According to the rule, he played with the team to which he was traded or he did not play at all.

Over the years, many players had spoken out on the unfairness of the rule. But no one had ever tried to change it—until Curt Flood. Risking his future in baseball, he chose to fight a system he was convinced was unfair. His teammates, friends, and even his family told him he was making a big mistake. Not only would his playing career end, he wouldn't even be hired as a coach or voted into the game's Hall of Fame.

While playing, eventually coaching, and one day being honored as one of the game's best were important to Flood, they were not as important as doing what his heart told him was right. For six long years, he fought major league baseball in the courts. And finally he won. It was ruled that players no longer had to go to a team they didn't want to. Instead, they were given the right to go to the team that made them the most attractive offer.

Curt Flood's courageous stand improved the life of every professional athlete to come after him. Long after his uniform number and batting average are forgotten, his unselfish contribution to others will long be remembered.

Those who not only accomplish great things but freely share the moment with others are the ones who can be assured a place in the history books. No athlete sets a record or wins a championship alone. Many others—family, friends, coaches, and teammates-play a part in such success.

The 1998 major league baseball season was the most fascinating I've ever followed—because of two great individual performances. The sports world looked on in awe as my old Southern Cal teammate, Mark McGwire of the St. Louis Cardinals, and Sammy Sosa of the Chicago Cubs slugged it out for the new record for home runs in a single season. Along the way, they displayed a degree of sportsmanship and respect for the game that warmed the hearts of fans across the country. Theirs was a friendly rivalry. When McGwire hit his sixty-second home run, breaking a 37-year-old record held by former New York Yankee great Roger Maris, one of the first to congratulate him was Sosa. Repeatedly, McGwire—who ultimately ended the season with an amazing 70 home runs to Sosa's 66—had told the press he felt it would be great for the season-long race to end in a tie. Mark and Sammy's mutual respect provided a great example of what sportsmanship is all about.

That respect was shared by millions of fans who followed the historic season. What they saw was a competition between two outstanding athletes, filled with great displays of class and humility. When Mark broke the historic record, the children of

the late Roger Maris were watching. After circling the bases, McGwire went into the stands and shared the moment with them, taking time to acknowledge their father and allow them to share in the glory of the moment. It was one of the

MUHAMMAD ALI

"The Greatest" started boxing at age 12. At age 18, he won a gold medal at the Olympics in Rome. Ali knocked out the reigning champion, Sonny Liston, in the first round of a match in 1965, to become the new champion.

most impressive moments in sports I've ever seen.

These are the things that being a hero is all about. Like Curt Flood and Jackie Robinson, they do things with their lives that benefit others. Like Muhammad Ali, they hold firmly to what they believe is right. Like Mark McGwire and Sammy Sosa, they bring pure joy to the sport they play, maintaining a strong sense of family, faith, and sportsmanship as they perform nearly incredible feats.

If you take time to look, you will find that our world is filled with such people. They are not all sports heroes or movie stars or great musicians. You see them daily in your own neighborhood. They are loving mothers and fathers who do all they can to protect and provide for you. They are the teachers and pastors devoted to helping prepare you for life in the adult world. They are your friends and neighbors who, in their own small ways, make the world a better place in which to live. You won't see their pictures on the covers of magazines or watch them running for touchdowns on national television. But they stand as wonderful examples just the same.

See what they do and listen to what they have to say, and I'm sure you'll agree with me.

CURT FLOOD

Flood played for the St. Louis Cardinals from 1956 to 1969. He hit over .300 six times and won seven Gold Gloves. He refused to be traded to the Phillies in 1969, and challenged baseball's reserve clause all the way to the Supreme Court, where he lost his case in 1972.

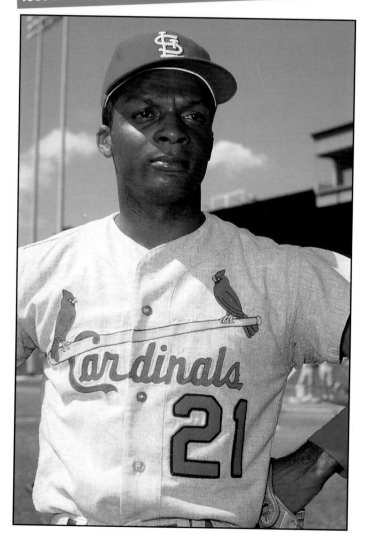

MARK McGWIRE   SAMMY SOSA

Mark McGwire and Sammy Sosa helped reenergize professional baseball in the 1998 season in their race to beat Roger Maris's 37-year-old single season record of 61 home runs. McGwire beat the record, but both players were honored for the mutual respect and admiration that they showed for each other.

STRENGTH OF THE HEART

4 DRINKING AND DRUGS

THE SADDEST EXPERIENCES I KNEW during my career in professional football were the funerals I attended. There have been too many of them. While the death of a friend is always hard to deal with, it is even harder when he dies so young—and for senseless reasons.

The list of people I've known who have died because of drug use or driving while drunk is a long one. And every time it happened I found myself asking a question for which I still have no satisfactory answer: Why?

Why did they throw away a promising future? Why did they do such damage to mind and body? Why did they hurt those who loved them by acting so foolishly? Why did they throw away their self-respect and the respect of others for the short-term feel-good sensation of alcohol or drugs?

If I had a good answer, maybe I could better understand what happened to Stacey Toran, my friend and Raiders teammate.

A strong safety, Stacey had been playing pro ball for six years. Through hard work, he had reached a level where others in the league were taking notice of his ability. Everything in his life seemed to be going well. He had a nice home with a wonderful view of the ocean. He was becoming a successful businessman. He was engaged to be married.

It was also important to him to be accepted by his teammates. Stacey wanted to prove that he was "one of the boys."

For years the Raiders had a tradition that never really appealed to me. One evening each week, the guys on the team would meet for dinner and drinks. The supposed purpose of these gatherings was to bring the team closer together. I went a few times myself. But when I saw that the real purpose seemed to be a contest to see who could drink the most beer, I decided there were better ways to spend my evenings. Stacey, however, was among those who felt it important to be there.

I wish he hadn't.

After one of those evening get-togethers at which he had had too much to drink, Stacey headed home in his car. Drunk and driving too fast, he tried to turn onto a highway exit and crashed into a concrete wall. He was not wearing a seat belt and was thrown thirty feet from the car. His skull was shattered. Doctors said he had probably died instantly.

When I heard the news the following day, I felt a numbing sadness and did something for which I have no real explanation. I drove to where the accident had occurred. Pulling over, I sat there for a long time, looking at the marks made by the impact of Stacey's car. There were still pieces of broken glass scattered on the roadside. Finally, I looked up the road. I could see his house, no more than a couple of hundred yards away. He had been so close to home. So close to safety. So close to being able to continue with his career and his life.

Stacey was a good person, but he made a tragic mistake in judgment. The same was true of Lyle Alzado, another of my teammates during my days with the Raiders.

Even before I met Lyle I was aware of his outstanding ability. He had been an All-Pro defensive lineman with the Denver Broncos, helping them get to the Super Bowl in 1978. No one in the game played with more all-out effort. He was one of the best. There was no doubt that the Raiders defense greatly improved when he became a member of our team. His presence was a big factor in our winning Super Bowl XVIII.

One of the first things we noticed when Lyle joined us was his unpredictable mood swings. He would be quiet and friendly one day, angry and ready to fight everybody the next. You never knew if he was going to be happy and easygoing or depressed and mad at the world. One day in practice he slammed a forearm against my head so hard I saw stars. It was a cheap shot, and I let him know it. Later, he apologized. But it would not be the last time he was violent with members of the team.

The case of Lyle's strange behavior was really no secret. Though he would not admit it, he was using steroids.

While using steroids was against league rules, Lyle Alzado was not the only one doing it. During my career I reached a point where I could pick the players who took drugs to improve their strength and muscles. Normally, a back my size can block a much larger lineman or linebacker by using the proper leverage. You just have to get low enough and have the right angle. But there were times when nothing worked. The bodies of some defenders I tried to block seemed steel-plated. They were using steroids to gain an unfair advantage.

Lyle was one of those players. But when our team doctor warned him of the health dangers of steroids, Lyle denied that he was taking them. A few years after his playing career ended, however, he became very ill.

His once-magnificent body turned to skin and bones. He lost his eyesight. Doctors told him he had brain cancer and was dying.

At this point Lyle did something far more courageous than anything he had ever done on the playing field. He publicly admitted the mistake he had been making for so long. Yes, he said, he had pumped thousands of dollars' worth of steroids and amphetamines into his body. For success as an athlete, he had sacrificed his health. The fame and fortune he wanted so badly destroyed his judgment—and his life.

Lyle Alzado died at the age of forty-three, certain that drug use had shortened his life.

The Raiders had a defensive end who was even bigger and stronger than Alzado. His name was John Matuszak, and he looked like a combination of Paul Bunyan and Grizzly Adams. He was six feet eight inches tall and weighed almost three hundred pounds. Rushing opposing quarterbacks, he was unstoppable. But off the field, his life was constantly out of control. Despite the efforts of teammates to convince him to take better care of himself, John seemed determined to self-destruct. He was arrested for drunk driving and possession of marijuana. He was once rushed to the hospital near death after drinking too much and taking too many sleeping pills. He never seemed to learn from his experiences.

Then, at the age of thirty-eight, he had a heart attack and died. The doctors said his death was the result of too much alcohol and too many pills. John had convinced himself that something bad could never happen to him. He was too big and strong, too macho. He would control his drinking and drug use. He thought he was smarter than those who tried repeatedly to warn him that he was on a destructive path.

He was dead wrong.

Since I have never used drugs or alcohol, it is difficult for me to understand why others do. I have heard all the excuses: "It makes me feel good."…"My troubles go away when I'm drinking or doing drugs."…"Everyone else is doing it."

What I haven't heard often enough are the honest facts. Smoking marijuana or snorting cocaine or shooting heroin is against the law. So is driving while intoxicated. Drugs and alcohol can do great damage to your mind and body. They can even kill you.

I guarantee you if Stacey Toran or Lyle Alzado or John Matuszak were still around today, they would agree. Lyle would have gladly exchanged his prized Super Bowl ring for good health. Stacey would rather have been a husband and father than a professional football player who was "one of the boys." John, too, would have liked a second chance to live his life differently. I'm convinced they would each say that they made the most terrible decisions of their lives when they drank their first beer, lit up their first joint, or took their first pill.

When I was in high school I knew kids were drinking and selling and using drugs. I saw even more of this when I got to college. And, yes, there were those who found it strange that I refused to take a drink or experience the "high" of smoking a joint or putting cocaine up my nose.

If they wanted to criticize me, that was their business. If they thought I wasn't "cool" or "with it," I didn't let it bother me. What I did was make a point of avoiding those I knew to be involved in such activities. Not that I was worried someone might finally tempt me to do something I didn't want to. I just didn't want to be associated with them. I didn't want to be "one of the boys" if it meant doing something I didn't believe in.

I knew if I was going to become the kind of athlete I hoped to be, it was important to do everything possible to see that my body and mind were in good condition. Alcohol and drugs would have defeated all my hard work. Also, I've always wanted to be aware of everything that was going on around me. I want to be in control of any situation I find myself in, both socially and during important games. That would be impossible if my mind were clouded.

If a friend couldn't accept that and understand why I didn't want to drink or do drugs, he wasn't much of a friend in the first place. Peer pressure is not an easy thing to deal with. But I've always felt that real respect comes from having the courage not always to go along with the crowd.

A friend of mine who speaks to a lot of school-age kids, warning them of the dangers of making a wrong decision about drugs, has offered one of the best and simplest pieces of advice I've heard.

"It's all about making the right decisions," he says. "If someone asks you to do something that you think might be harmful to you, stop for a few seconds and ask yourself these questions.

"How will what I'm thinking about doing affect me?

"How will it affect my friends? My family? Those I love and those who love me?"

The questions are not difficult. Nor does it take a genius to come up with the right answers.

5 TEAMWORK

SINCE MY RETIREMENT AS A PLAYER, I have spent a lot of time thinking back over my career, looking for that one special moment that best explains the feeling I have about sports, a shining example of the determination and teamwork that is so necessary for success.

It came in my first season with the Kansas City Chiefs. We were playing a very good Houston Oilers team for the 1993 division championship and leading by just one point with only a couple of minutes left.

The game had been an exhausting dogfight, and every Chiefs player—offense, defense, special teams—had given everything they had. We were all running on empty, yet still doing everything we could to hold on for the victory we so badly wanted. But if we were to win, our offense had to continue moving the ball and keep it away from a dangerous Oilers attack.

As we had done so often during the game, we found ourselves facing a critical third-down situation. We had to make just one more first down to be sure that time would run out before Houston got a

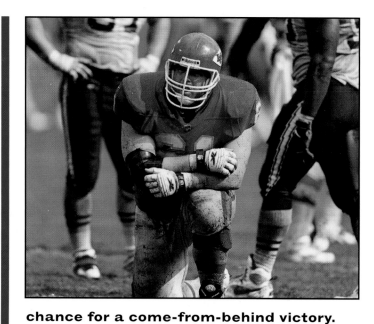

blocking I've ever seen opened a hole for me, and I was able to run twenty yards for a touchdown that sealed our victory over the favored Oilers.

The fact that I was the scorer is not my reason for telling this story. It is the determination and intensity Tim Grunhard displayed that Sunday afternoon. What he was feeling as we stood in the huddle is exactly what everyone who has ever seriously competed

chance for a come-from-behind victory.

As we huddled it was not our All-Pro quarterback, Joe Montana, who first spoke. Nor was it me. It was Tim Grunhard, our three-hundred-pound center, who rarely said anything during the course of a game. He was bruised and exhausted. His uniform was spotted with blood. Sweat poured down his face, as he looked at each of us through the bars of his battle-scarred helmet.

"Look, guys," he shouted, clenching his fists as he spoke, "I'm no big star. I'm just a guy from Chicago who has never won anything in his life. I want this so bad! Help me out there. Let's do what we've got to do to win this thing!"

On the very next play, some of the best

in sports has felt. No personal sacrifice is too great, once you've set your sights on a goal. You forget your aches and pains. You forget you're so tired your lungs feel like they're on fire. What you concentrate on is the responsibility you have to those playing alongside you.

Unless you are a die-hard Kansas City Chiefs fan, you probably never heard of Tim Grunhard. Few offensive centers, even in the NFL, are household names. But the quest for victory was every bit as important to him as it was to the star quarterback or the running back who scored the touchdowns. If a team is to succeed, it must have Tim's determined spirit spread from one end of the roster to the other.

I have great admiration for those athletes who participate in individual sports. The ability and courage of boxers Muhammad Ali and Sugar Ray Leonard, training alone and then stepping into the ring to fight their way to a championship, is remarkable. The concentration and skill of golfer Tiger Woods, carefully making every shot as perfect as possible and winning the Masters, blew me away. Watching sprinter Michael Johnson, a picture of incredible speed and determination, race down the homestretch in 1996 to win Olympic gold

medals in the 200 and 400 meters earned my great admiration.

But for me, nothing beats the thrill of being part of a team effort, sharing the excitement of competition with others who have the same goal.

I have always admired the sheer beauty of football. I know this seems like a strange way to describe a sport that is so violent. But if you stop and think about it, the game is much more than a bunch of guys running around, knocking each other down. Played right, it has a poetry all its own. It demands style and grace, strength and speed. It teaches hard lessons about success and failure, joy and disappointment.

shown the courage to stand in the pocket, patiently waiting for me to get open, I would have caught very few passes. If the defense doesn't do its job, the offense doesn't get the opportunity to put points on the scoreboard.

My name may have been in the headlines a lot. The television highlights might have shown me diving into the end zone for a touchdown. But I never in my life won a game by myself. The team won because everyone did the job assigned to him.

I liked being part of that. It is a feeling that not only comes when one reaches the professional level, it is there for those who compete in the peewee leagues and for their high school teams.

Though it is a game, it offers a wonderful classroom in which to learn lessons that will be valuable for a lifetime. Think about it. During the course of one afternoon you are forced to make one decision after another. You make mistakes and have to overcome them as quickly as possible. Your courage is tested over and over. You depend on your teammates, just as they are looking for help from you.

You share something with those who have sweated alongside you. To me, that unique kinship was what made playing the

Not only do you learn responsibility to your fellow players, you learn how important their help is to you.

The most important lesson football offers is this: No team will ever be really outstanding unless all its members are dedicated to doing their very best.

On game days I might have to had run for a lot of yardage. But if my blockers hadn't been giving every ounce of effort they had, there would have been no place for me to go. If the quarterback hadn't game special. I was fortunate to be on a number of good teams during my career. What made them good was the fact that we worked together like a family that genuinely cared for one another.

In my final season with the Chiefs, we traveled to Oakland for a Monday Night Football game against the Raiders. I knew it would be the last time I played on the home field of my old team, and I wanted to do well. My adrenaline was really pumping—maybe too much.

At a critical point in the game, with the Raiders ahead, I fumbled the ball as we were driving for a touchdown. Jogging to the sidelines, I was in agony, feeling I had let the game slip away from us. But then, with just eleven seconds left to play, our quarterback, Elvis Grbac, threw a long pass to wide-receiver Andre Rison. Andre made a spectacular catch for a touchdown that gave us a 28–27 victory.

I rushed onto the field, hugging players, thanking everyone I could find for what they had done to overcome the mistake I had made earlier in the game. In the dressing room, after all the celebration finally died down, the coaches presented Andre with the game ball for his outstanding performance.

With cheers ringing through the room, Andre walked over to me and smiled. "I know how important this game was to you," he said, and he pitched the game ball to me. "I want you to have it."

I've received more than my share of game balls over the years, but none more special than that one. Andre's gesture demonstrated everything good about being part of a team.

6 DISCUSSION QUESTIONS

How important was it that Marcus listened to the lessons taught him by his parents when he was a youngster?

1

_____
_____
_____
_____
_____
_____
_____
_____
_____
_____
_____

Did the high school coach do the right thing when he dismissed Marcus from the team?

_____
_____
_____
_____
_____
_____
_____
_____
_____

Who are the adults you would talk with if you had a problem?

_____
_____
_____
_____
_____

Who are the people you know personally who have shown the qualities of a hero or role model? Make a list.

_____
_____
_____
_____
_____
_____

STRENGTH OF THE HEART

5

Do you think Marcus would have been such a successful athlete if he had decided it was okay to drink and use drugs?

_____
_____
_____
_____
_____
_____
_____

6

What would you do if you went to a party and found people using alcohol and drugs?

_____
_____
_____
_____
_____
_____
_____

7

Why do you think young people your age make the decision to experiment with drinking and drugs?

_____
_____
_____
_____
_____
_____
_____

8

Do you stop to think how your own actions affect others? Make a list of everyone who would be disappointed if you got in trouble with the law.

_____
_____
_____
_____
_____
_____
_____
_____

9

What are the most important questions you would like to ask someone you admire and respect?

_____
_____
_____
_____
_____
_____
_____
_____

10

What are your goals in life?

_____
_____
_____
_____
_____
_____

STRENGTH OF THE HEART